THE MIRROR
AT THE TOP OF
THE STAIRS

THE MIRROR
AT THE TOP OF
THE STAIRS

*Poems written
at the New Britain Museum of American Art*

Jonas Zdanys

BLACK SPRUCE PRESS

The Mirror at the Top of the Stairs, Poems Written at the New Britain Museum of American Art was published in Brooklyn, New York,
July, 2023 by Black Spruce Press.

Cover image:
Night
Earth and Reflection Moon
John Haberle
c. 1909
Oil on board
79 x 52 in.
Gift of Mr. and Mrs. Victor Demmer
New Britain Museum of American Art, 1966.66

Design by Regina Schroeder

blacksprucepress.org
blacksprucepress@gmail.com
Manufactured in the United States of America

*In memory of my 11TH grade honors English teacher
at New Britain High School,
Steven T Florie, who encouraged us always
to have "the courage to be" and whose love of painting,
and of the New Britain Museum of American Art,
inspired me then and continue to inspire me now.*

Contents

The Mirror at the Top of the Stairs

I was once somebody else,
an old woman with curvature
of the spine playing the piano
in late afternoon in a weathered
house on a farm in Nebraska.
My children reorganized
the cupboards when I was
sleeping, smiling in every mirror
they passed by, pleased with
their wonders and tricks.
I did not think about happiness,
finding no truth in such ideas,
dyeing my hair black each year
and watching it grow out white
with the changing seasons.
No one took my word for it,
there was nothing else I could do,
these things don't mean that much,
these ritual labors and small rewards
of a world that seemed to be
the most casual imitation of events

on a far landscape, out in the country.
One spring, like blood from a stone,
water flooded the house, loosened
the tiles and warped the legs
of the piano. Someone painted
a sign on the door, a dark circle
with a line drawn through it,
like a spell to keep the light
intact, a defiance of circumstance
and death borrowed from some
random circle in the ground.
It was a reassuring, peaceful thing,
as if the present stretched on forever.
My expectations for myself ran along
the same lines, the same dark circles
covered my dress, and it all seemed
reasonable enough, it all boxed up
the world of which I was a part, though
I also admired bright colors and forms,
though I walked sometimes in too much light.

Seeing Wyeth's "McVey's Barn" Seventeen Years Later

[Andrew Wyeth, "McVey's Barn"]

In this place of memory
beneath a sky full of branches
ringed by the far-off hum
of cicadas, light powders
the quiet weave and dust
of straw. Shadows sprinkled
across the coarse boards
crumble like braids of dirt
tapped from dry roots.
A touch of pale color,
like shadings of brush stroke
or line, trembles above
the sleigh burrowed high
on the brown rafters, spreads
in the still afternoon air
like gray smoke, rising and
fading in the loose darkness
of this New England barn.

Small birds gather in the grass
and the blue jay's song lifts
across the narrow yard.
Your footsteps still echo
on these floorboards where we
danced naked that summer
thinking no one would see,
our bodies dusted with light
that filtered through the thin
barn walls with the sweet
smell of late roses. And though
half our lives have passed,
that afternoon has not left
this place, locked in the warm
smells of barn straw and flowers
and dappling the walls like
bird song or pale dust washed
by a haze of fragile light.
(1984)

4

Late Courtship

There is nothing he can do
to hold it back, nothing to make
the stillness last forever, nothing
to keep the moment from coming
to an end.
Inside, there is a smell
of cooking down the dark hall
leading from the kitchen to the half-closed bedroom door,
a waft of cigarette smoke folds
again in the bed sheets. Her foot
touches his, a deliberate move
that turns inert and cold when
the clock strikes. The candle on
the table droops to a pool of wax.
Shoulders, hips, knees: he is drawn
to desire, tears at the edge of the white
dress. He wipes his mouth with his
cuff, his skin like paper, and waits.
His finger follows the loop of the chain
around her neck, moves to the cross
between her breasts. There is no sound

but the scrum of birds trapped in the loose folds of the awning.
Two inscriptions are stitched in the curtain.
He makes a separate peace.
He dies for truth.
He looks away.

That Summer
After Nijolė Miliauskaitė

[Joseph Badger, "Hannah Minot Moody"]

she wore light
long wide dresses
the wind carried her

down streets and through parks
easily, as if through a dream
with blossoming lindens

the thin soft cloth
did not hide
her breasts and in the sun
you could see her supple
young body

it was so hot

we rested
in wicker chairs
in the shade of giant
old trees, the river's reflections

glittered on our faces, boats
parasols and clouds floated gently by
in the distant gazebos lay opened books leafed
through by unseen hands

On Dark Sand

[Winslow Homer, "Ship's Boat"]

The ship struck the rocks on the far coast
gray as a mirror polished with slow care,
tired of the landscape of the sea and soundless
as a dream from which no one wakes.
The war blackened the windows, curved roads
leading nowhere and time beginning to drift
like the slow last breaths of sailors on the ocean.
The days contract, blind with their own hard
light, and the nights grow colder. Stars litter the sea.
Clouds are a stiff brush on the horizon.
Something with three wings hovers above the sand,
shivers in slow strokes over dark flowers.
The searchlights fall, the wind wears north,
the air hollows to an inexorable warning.
A hand thrusts upwards from among the reeds.
The iron rod of time bends like a candle in heat.

The Last of Her Kind

[Chao Chan, "Karenni Girl"]

All night I rolled rocks up
and down the slope of the hill,
the grass below transparent,
the dark gray sky at dead rest.
The girl with the skirt over her
head sat on a bench watching,
half-trapped and muffled
in multi-colored cloth. Her legs were bent
as she unbuttoned her blouse,
bold and white, and then stiffened
her arm. She felt cold and tired,
a strip of blackness just beyond
her hands, a great silence angling
the bottom of the air like the bitter
aftertaste of love. The sum of these
events is undrawn, the point of the
periphery of a world made and
unmade by the changing stones.
The moment is over.

I performed all the rites.
What is mine on this hill
belongs to no one, what is hers
on the bench belongs to me.

When God Relents

[Helen Frankenthaler, "Solar Imp"]

She asked how long it would take
until God relented, her youngest
son holding the dog by its tail
and asking for the world to be forgiven.
Or at least come to its beginning again
on some long and solemn afternoon
when children kneel in their corners
waiting for the touch of a phantom
hand and reciting the sufferings
of people asleep in other rooms.
Death is not the measure of all things,
they say, imagining the wild waters.
The cup will fill in time, they say,
in the passion of surrender.
At midnight the dog whines softly,
the boy's grip tightening, and she
wakes once more, hears the high
and silent slide of night,
the tremor of derision
at last in God's exhausted voice.

Gray Rain on the Far Banks

[Stevan Dohanos, "Rained-In Vacationers"]

The boat plunges across the East River
dragging a gray rain to the far bank,
a blue haze locked in a cool summer as
the city sags weightless against the horizon.
The boat is finally gone, morning taking
its own time, slouched on a stone bench.
The lives of old men slow to mourn
dull to a cold simplicity and the dock
slides away to the dust of rutted streets.
Life is familiar as a scar. Below the limestone
and granite of the bridge a boy's body
spreads out, face down,
and out on the rocks
someone stands holding onto a kite string.
Past the pier, to the left of the landing,
there were people walking,
sails on the water red and blue.
Someone could fall here unnoticed.
Someone could slide quietly into the water
and not stir the air, arms pressing no
darkness aside, float for a thousand years

in the silence of the setting moon.
Someone could sleep and die alone.
This is what I saw today east of the island.
This is what I saw today in the white
shadows of the city.

Twilight Dance

[Mary Ellen Andrews, "George Deem, Head of a Girl by B.A.
and George Deem by M.E., 1966"]

The light in the kitchen of the house
next door goes out. They are suddenly
blind, trembling to undress, caught
in the sounds of things before the storm.
They stumble in the dark in small circles
hoping to find each other again,
one foot—her right, his left—nailed
loosely to the wide planks of the wooden
floor, each arm waving the thick darkness
away. It was a moment neither
wished to keep, the measure of all things,
of anguish, of lack, knocking on the window,
falling to a gray dust that coats the walls.
The moon is obscured but I can see
the shadows of their odd dance.
I am looking for a way out for them,
my hand half-raised, time standing
still, my heart misbeating. She flaps her
arms like a painted bird in response,
fluttering toward the ceiling, pulled back

by the nail in the floor.
He strikes a match.
There is a sudden rush of air.

Through Darkened Glass
[Georgia O'Keefe, "East River From the 30th floor of the Shelton Hotel, 1928"]

The dark-skinned boy in the window
of the tenement building just past
the tracks on the way into the city
rummages through the sounds he hears
on the stairway, his clothes damp
with the burden he carries with him
through the world. When the day
of judgment comes he will feel no
mercy for the world of unrelieved
night, the birds frozen in the air in
mid-flight in a posture he cannot forget,
the corner of the moon broken
against the water tower's spiral drift.
The postcard I bought at the station
when the train arrived showed a boy
running through a small park along the river between
high walls, his face averted, an imaginary
scene devoid of expression in some
distant country grown old and gray.
I'm not sure if it's the same boy
I saw from the train, some settled

story told in one brief moment
when the day grows dim
and the invisible things of the world burst
enigmatic to the truth that overwhelms us.
I believe yet don't believe
what I am saying: he falls vertically from the window,
runs thrashing through the rush of cold air,
hides his face with his back to the street
and quells premonitions of his own panic
as he gropes his way to the last flight
of stairs.
Truth comes in winding ways.
It is like a wisp of smoke
in the corner of a postcard found in
a scattered pile on a folding table
outside the station.
There is something else looming in
that picture.
Some shapes of it can
only be seen through darkened glass.

Old Lady Sewing

This allegory of faith
and innocent desire is a soft
moment brooding through leaded glass,
dissolved contours of a world in composed balance,
all purity and harmony, concentrated and clear
in the strands
of dark thread that fall across the white fabric
and onto her shaded lap, her face
consecrated with the sanctity of simple
pleasures as if life itself was gathering up at last
to embrace her, the significance of something as ordinary
as a white cloth
to be put to honest use—

simple things and simple actions in her life treasured as divine gifts,
and the light enters her and she draws
breath again, the breath of truth, obligation,

and piety, and in Eakins's hands,
when she is gone, this is her life,
waiting for the passage that grows no lighter, no darker, framed forever

in stillness and shade,
never moving, as the days pass, from that
scene to mystery or transcendence, her soul
showing through the flesh, beyond the farthest void,
the distillation and fate of her duty, the deep down
stirring of the knowledge a woman alone has.
I think of her when I lie in bed at night and stare
into the dark hole into which I am falling.
I wonder if she is an angel come to show me
the way out. She goes before and I follow,
my eyes shut in order to see.

Only the Moment is Eternal

[John Haberle, "Time and Eternity" ca 1889]

It's hard to know how to fill up
your days and keep them near
at hand when you know that something
is going to crack open, an unexpected
noise from the deeper silence of a broken
watch that startles you awake to some
riddled end when the rest of the house
is bare and sleeping and undone.
The hours swell without remorse
then shrink down
while a coldness grows
and your face lapses like a darkened star.
The year is a patch of dry land cut by
empty ravines.
Dark moths ring
the far edges of the world.
Time hangs by a thin chain
in a bag dropped in a ditch by the side
of the road, longs to run in the straits
where unfamiliar noises bloom.
I'm at a loss.

The sound takes down
its own debris and the great work
is done in other places, in other, closely-held moments.
I would lie to you if I could.

When the River Empties

You can stand at the edge of the river
in late October as the sun sets and hold
the whole world in your hand. In the middle
of night you can hear the thin sweet
voice of the river emptying into the sea,
rocks slipping into water and the wind
coming up like some miraculous thing
finding constant shape. The sky is clear,
an oblique harmony of currents and pulses
in great migration west. I hear birds
vanishing, something unknown rising
and falling in the offshore surges.
There is a point of rest for us all, the balance
between the many and the one, the unity
of substance and abstraction in the white
curve of the tide. Everything here breaks
to possibility, the soft white in heaven's eye.
An immaculate morning will rise.

Just Past the Fence

[Grace Albee, "The Bogen Place"]

I.
Nobody comes here to stay:
footprints disappear at the turn
of the walk, at the edge of the yard,
in the changing soil, near the posts and stones.
Ideas of permanence flutter by,
fuse in the weeds and gravel like unraveled bird bones
anticipating every random event.
The moon moves only when I move,
rising from the ground and tumbling
down the edges of the dark road. Bricks flake
above my head, the window glass
rattles. The dead sing in my sleep.
This is how memory is made,
groping like a hand on a cold wall.
Dim lights illuminate both, the end of
each hall blocked by a closed door.
How still she keeps herself, the heavy
posture, unlightened by motion,
generating its own uncertainty,
various truths that cannot be reconciled

at the center of any possibility.
Something summons itself, wanting
to be healed. Something remembers,
something knocks again on the door.

2.
It was an odd gesture,
an uncalculated act.
He lies down fully clothed,
rocks from side to side, touches himself,
imagining her,
because he is unable to fall asleep.
The day is cut from stone.
The confusion of the world
is like the wagging of a burned
finger on the other side
of the room: he is his own
father now, a new double
under a dust-gray light.
He closes his eyes, his mind
on other things, his father's
letter on the table written
in his own resilient hand,
addressed to himself.

A sudden noise confuses him.
He crosses the threshold.
History comes to an end.
All things are permitted,
he knows, and falls silent
and fevered onto his bed.
It's better, he thinks, to sleep.

3.

He had been drinking and came home
in the middle of the night, his mind
wandering like a seizure across no world
he knows. He travels through a wide plain.
Lightning flashes like something reinvented
in the hands of sober men.

4.

In that quick light, he sees that on the grassy knoll
just past the fence
at the end of the yard
stands a woman with a dead child in her arms,
no look of surprise or alarm on her face,
just the image of a faint smile, cold and
brittle as drifting smoke, framed by her

falling hair.
there is not much else to bear the quick necessities.
As the sun rises, the hour strikes its end.
A moment of silence opens a moment of silence.
Time reverses the vision of time.

5.
His voice rises, he rubs his eyes,
unsure of what is swallowed in the dark.
He is not sure if he should plead for himself
or call out to the dumb weight at the end of the world
and then turns because it doesn't matter.

6.
He is here today, will be gone tomorrow, like wind
forcing itself through the seams of the fence at night,
the isolation of the heart carried down to an unkept yard
along an unnamed road in an anonymous town.

7.
The glass in the windows above his head is black.
He can feel the child's soft bones fold.
Things are not entirely as they appear,
a sad business that the man writing something at the table

shakes his head over, nothing to do
but call to God to save him
as he wanders on stiff wings across a dark horizon of anticipated rain.
The air below the chimney smells of ash and cold soot,
his eyes are full of remorse,
fixed on the night and the promise of water.

Digital Images

[Shantell Martin, "Digital Image"]

Black water breaks through the ceiling
and the rafters creak with their own truth,
rain somber and drumming the roof.
There was a point at which I awoke, sure
that I had the power to predict the future,
the drops of rain not twelve inches apart.
I started with the past, decided to bring
it down to zero, half a year at a time at first
and then faster and faster until I reached
the perfection of nothing. From there
I could shape whatever next moment I wanted,
skipping the decades I did not know, ignoring
centuries like unwelcome guests or strangers
huddled and dangerous. I feel the fingers of time
groping me, searching for memories that
have not existed, for the source of any image
that has not yet afflicted the world.
I won't allow it, won't spend the night
flapping the bed sheets to shake out
the truths and lies that will once again be
new on the face of the earth, won't fret

for any incomprehensible penance that
shapes the shadows of love. And in this
version of my new beginning, when courage
and resolution are put to the test, God will
be a splay-footed old lesbian in a wheelchair wearing a gait belt
and holding up a cardboard sign
that she will work for shelter or food,
a pint of muscatel, cheap wine in a jug.
History moves quickly once it gets moving,
frames the meaning I cannot bring myself to tell.
I wait for the rain to be falling again,
I start the clock backwards to zero.

How Are We Remembered?

The wall in the center of the square,
just past the gray Civil War monument,
is chalked with the names of anonymous
boys who leave the quick pulses of their
lives behind in widening arcs. It was a
sense of triumph, a moment of power
off the main road, that rumpled their
lonely wisdom and gave shape to their
belief that their lives were the only lives
to live. There was no other way to go in.
But the old bones buried here longer
than anyone remembers feel a different
longing, not the eternal now scratched
insolently on a rock but the notch
of the past etched on the barrel by a soldier
who fights for his life as his years contract
and his name is smothered away from home in dirt and blood.
Not a footprint remains in the empty grass
in whatever field this marble tried to save.
Only the name in red of some local boy
sprayed on the pigeoned pedestal. The

clouds of summer hang like dogs in the square.
The world steadies like an unmourned
grave. The angel at the top of the statue
whispers light on a passing girl's face.

When the War Ended

[Peter Waite, "Bridge"]

She took the train across
the green rusting bridge, the houses
just beyond the tracks, in the
heat of those days, ruins left
by swarms of bombers
that came all night, that
juggled the landscapes
to unfamiliar destinations.
She traveled alone, bed on board,
on the way to see her sister,
the corruption of that war held still
where time was no longer content.
The night settled to three,
the shadows at each passing station
no solace for the hand or eye.
In the strange city, the lights
were out, a terrible darkness
on each face she saw. A horse-drawn
cart stood crippled near the tower.
The unrecoverable waste of history
loosed upon the changing images

of time suffered and moved, hung
like a yellow moon from a darkening
cloud and crushing the crescent
pressures of every life it wrecked.
Her sister, stripped naked, lay
salvaged to ruin by its intolerable stare.
She turned away when the train began
to move again, the night, for her, forever on the hills.

Toward a Philosophy of Goodness

[John Singleton Copley, "Lydia Lynde"]

She asked that I believe in goodness
and I replied that all beliefs are tentative.
It was an unpretentious life, no majestic
meanings swept up from under the rug,
no grand design that others watched.
Only the joy of subversive acts in the small
middle of things, the integers lost
as I drew my face on the cold glass with a puff
of warm air. It was not all just idle chatter.
It was not all just obscure philosophies that tug
themselves loose from the curtains and shawls.
I'm aware that the struggle has never ceased.
The man with the lamp in his hand
on the street shudders without reason
or cause. He murmurs a word or two
about goodness, counts out his steps
backwards along the inner wall.
The question she asked did not disconcert
him, did not keep the next sentence from
passing his lips. He gathers his wits all
about him, fixes his gaze on her breasts.

Iron Wings Rising in the Fog

[Judith Allen-Efstathiou, "Summer Fog"]

In a dark alley shrouded in fog, the flame sawed and the day
lashed and the ghosts on the rooftops
stirred. All of them are gone except
for me, the iron ascending when black
birds flicker in the scales of their long
descent. It was where the street turned
left off the main road, near the edge
of town where the roofs were flat
and the windows long and the houses
narrow and bare. The floor creaked when
I went outside to listen to the voices
that gathered in that other night,
my cold hand inching across the barren
circles, the dust on the stairs pushing
words into my mouth in response.
There was something past the statue
in the square, a shadow floating
in the moonlight, the night holding
its breath, that led me to an empty
space pinned against the light.
A single word floated up from the iron of the past.

An unpredictable scrawl numbed the moon.
I stood to let the darkness rise.
And I was falling, falling, like a meager wall,
falling bleak when the street rebelled, and
when I turned, transfixed, iron wings took hold.

Instead

[Joseph Goldyne "The Attic with Pillow:
Het Achterhuis/Anne Frank/Diary of a Young Girl"]

She had begun to live in memory,
lay yellowed photographs out across
the kitchen table, read old unrequited love letters
saved in bent brown folders, tried to
find familiar yellow stars in lost constellations.
She understood then that it's hard at the outset to break
the boundary, to reach for shapes
to fill the space in the air made by a moving hand,
to hold what can be held
and then let go and float away free in a column of smoke.
The only epoch was her own.
She is a strange face in the attic window,
dull with loss and perplexed by the glare of the lights in the distance
that sweep
the horizons.
She is today the color of wind in a headland of rocks
gathered
and carried up the stairs to unbind the moon,
the things of her world are retrieved as if through a glass darkly
and piled in stacks on tables of stained wood.

38

The ellipse of the past folds a universe
of balance and risk into a savage now.
The present drives time gone
and to come spinning on its axis.
The girl's face even from here is ash and stone.
She used to tell me that she sometimes dreams
of going mad. Her voice is every shade
of gray, the synthesis and symbol of a
place under an old and darkening sky.
The night each night howls and sighs
as she trembles with the echoes of her walk across the attic,
presses her pillow to her hollows,
knows that she will never be filled.
Her fingers tap the moon in the window
on its dark gray brow, and she watches the dull knives of the universe
trim the last shapes of black paper to form the masters of time.
Every shadow on the street and walls folds to a
new myth freed from the innocence of her past.
This is the prophecy of her life in the attic,
the muddled ghost that waits
like the certainty she seeks.
She presses herself against the wall,
her voice constantly changing its hues,
and talks about the cold and the night that skids
across a temporary covenant of rooftops.

2.
The old man dressed in brown and green
leads the blind black horse down the street,
past the house where she stands looking out the attic window.
Children run
from the alley
across the way and chase
after the horse,
hitting its rump and sides with sticks
and leaf-covered branches.
The horse kicks its hind legs, catching a boy dressed in a black shirt
Square in his middle.
He falls and turns his head toward the window. They lock eyes as he points up at
the window and shouts out in a loud croak, struggling to catch his breath

—"face!"—
the horse snorts, startled,
and shakes its head,
reins pulling hard on the old man's hand.
He looks up and sees the face.

3.
It was well past the middle of his life,
some nervous splinter of what remained
under his skin—a shrug of forgiveness
ready for everyone who passed him by
on the street without looking up.
Some argued that he should move out
of there then, but he didn't like the bother
of moving, and there was more to it
than that: each night he heard the telephone next door
ring three times and then stop as the earth
went on spinning and the first light in the hallway came on.
He didn't know
how it all came to be, but it was enough.
A red bird once paused on the sill of his kitchen window,
just as twilight fell, and he sat in his corner
like a flaw in the painted wood, rising lightly to
a small scatter. That hid him from the brown and green that was his life.
All he asked was to stay alive. All he asked.
That was something he wanted to tell her:

That his horse-reined fingers would not toss her life away,
even if they threatened to dissolve him in one of those places in the east he heard
                                        others talk about.

After all, he thought, it was not he but the boy who saw the face and shouted.
Instead, he wanted to fold his voice with hers in the cracks of the walls of the attic.
Listen to how she whispered both their names through the window to the boy
lying on the sidewalk
and to the horse stamping in the street.
he would, instead, in time become the shadow of smoke from the east,

stealing across the reflection
in the window of her face, on its way west.

About the Author

Jonas Zdanys is the author of fifty-five other books. They include collections of his poetry written in English or in Lithuanian and volumes of his translations into English of Lithuanian poetry and fiction. He is also editor of several anthologies, among them collections of found poetry, epistolary poetry and, most recently contemporary surrealist and magical realist poetry. He serves currently as Poet in Residence and Professor Emeritus of English at Sacred Heart University.

www.ingramcontent.com/pod-product-compliance
Lightning Source LLC
Chambersburg PA
CBHW040218110726
48005CB00019B/3064